Sweet Oleander
A Collection of Poetry
by Chanel Hardy

I0626582

Create.
even when the world is falling apart
because when the dust clears and the terror
subsides
someone will pick up this book beneath the
rubble
and smile.

-A Message to the Reader
Love, Chanel.

Stranded

Being a socially conscious Black creator is like being stuck in the desert with nothing to drink. You walk for hours in the smoldering heat with nothing but your thoughts to keep you busy. You feel like giving up. All hope seems lost. Until you see the silhouette of someone in the distance. You muster up what's left of your energy and run to them, hoping it's not a mirage. You let out a sigh of relief and in front of you stands a woman. Beautiful and polished, holding a cup as she smiles. You grab the cup from her hands, and as you take a sip you realize it's steaming hot chocolate. You spit it out, she disappears and your shoulders slump as you drop the cup. The disappointment hurts. But this wasn't the first time and it won't be the last. All we can do is keep going. On our journey to spread truth, encouragement, love and acceptance. Continuing on your endless trek for something real. Someone who understands your plight. Our journey is far from over.

I Had a Dream About You

but not the kind you'd expect

as a matter of fact,
I don't think it was a dream at all
because if it was, I'd wake up
so here I sit, still.

still waiting for the fog to clear
still waiting for my mind to reset back to
sequence one

the one where I'm alive
and there are still finger smudges on the
walls
and dust in the corners
and crust in my eyes

truth is, I don't know what this is
but I remember what life tastes like
I remember that
I remember what it's like to live

Black Lives Matter

She asks for milk for her burning eyes
but all you hear are burning fires

tone-deaf sympathy about death and broken
windows
glass shards in black skin
black blood on pavement

gaslighting fires that started long before any
protest told you we couldn't breathe.

Anatomy of a Poem (Prose Poem)

I never realized how similar poetry and sex were, until I took the time to fully undress in front of an audience. Whether it be on a page, or on a stage. Showing your ass, literally or metaphorically requires thick skin, and a level of vulnerability that most people don't see outside of the bedroom. To allow your mind and body to go to sacred spaces. Untouched places. When someone writes a poem, they're asking you to look at them. To give them your full attention and admire what you came for. Or paid for. People, say that being a poet isn't a real job because I guess a real job requires that you use your body. But those same people also say that sex work isn't a real job, because people with real jobs don't use their bodies. But I say, being a poet requires skill. Because it takes skill to show the most intimate parts of yourself to complete strangers. If you look at the anatomy of a poem, you'll see the human body in four parts

The heart, the brain, the lungs and muscle. All things that make life possible. If you take one of those away, all you're left with is an empty shell of a person. And If you look at the anatomy of a person you'll see a poem grouped into six separate stanzas. Sex is an elegy, a tribute to the human body. A ballad about the human experience that bears your children. Poetry is a privilege.

What have you done to deserve this body?

A War Poem

I can see them through the window
hear their screams through the walls
feel the heat through the cracks
my cup quivers
the chandelier shakes
the room rattles
my heart races because they beg for mercy
my heart settles when they stop
my heart hurts because there is none.

Coldest Winter Ever

She's the type of female jumping to
conclusions
too quick
without knowing the ones who seen it all

nobody's shit ain't real anyway
sob stories and snow storms
so proud I got a diamond
gold fingers, soft, no slum
cheap real thing

three, four, a whole slew to worry about
reputation, common sense, family
and so on

sooner than later
she'll realize
it wasn't worth the royal red carpets.

Room for a Sinner

Mysterious eyes
a million faces
mysterious skin
take me places
I've never been
like sacred temples
ancient tombs
enclosed for the dead
but my spirit makes room
I suppose, there will be room for me
on the almighty's list
of the chosen and free
the perfect
pristine, clean
not like me
a mysterious thing
an unexplored vessel
of life in-between
a mysterious being
with no resting place
an untapped soul
trapped in a untapped space.

Passing

Ordinary letters
illegible alien
mysterious and slightly thin thing
not peculiar, a little flaunting
foreign, extraordinary postmarked brows
a tiny frown, perplexity from annoyance in
her thoughts
wholly unable to reveal the idea she
reflected
all that she knew always on the edge
aware but certainly not feeling outrage
for a swift moment sitting, sewing pieces
together
bellowing curses which were less
frightening
sometimes suggested that she had known
well enough
she made up her mind in spite of possible
danger
even in those days life beyond her
immediate desire was selfish
and yet, she had a strange passion
15 years old, lips pressed, arms folded
staring at the face of her disdain
and black eyes silent and staring, weeping
the outburst had begun
she glanced in a sharp flashing scorn
she vanished
the long stretch of years pent-up fury

grief, she had enough
certainly if any word could describe her, she
was rashly impulsive
and amazing
hidden well away, driven to anger.

Going out of Business

Paid the price with no profit
my mind was in the red
so I charged it
to the game that is
another loss, fuck it
we'll bounce back though
we always do
and they'll open up shop elsewhere
as always, that's how they move
tax exempt with no stake in the game
no shame
a soul proprietor with a trail of debt behind
you
a mountain of lies to climb
at the expense of black and brown bodies
and minds.

Love Reincarnated

The moon can't see
and the sun can't speak
the planets wither
they crumble and seep
into a deep black hole
until there's nothing left
just you and me
drifting apart as the universe empties
out all her baggage
and rebuilds from scratch
but even in the emptiest of spaces, love
never dies
so when the stars align
we can orbit back together
and in time
you'll find
another love like mine.

Royals

Fingers dipped in gold.
hands covered in me.
eyes smooth like honey
in your eyes I can see
a glimpse of your past lives
once upon a dream you were a king
you ruled across the seven seas
now you rule over me
a revolutionary, I was sent to kill you
"Off with his head!" they said
now I'm on your throne too
a sellout
I abandoned the resistance
but how could I resist you
resist this
your destructive kiss
pulled me in, now I'm queen of the damned
where my dignity once stood
a castle stands
but your reign is over
it's my kingdom now
now it's my head you want
"Long live the king!"
now take my crown.

UFO

The sun burns my skin
as the world turns
I gravitate towards the light
the sun sets
and the skies prepare for night
the air is cold, but I can see the light
I'm alone
but I can see the light
the entrance is warm
I'm closer now
not at home anymore
but still alone
somehow, he knows my name
all my troubles exposed
all my crimes
he knows why I'm here, but I don't
a specimen chosen by him
to cut open and explore
I've never been this open before
an experiment
an extraterrestrial whore
letting him in on all of earth's secrets
before he lets me go
And I descend back to earth again
back to life
past the sun, as it burns again
and I wonder
will he send for me again?

Monday Morning Blues

Summer truly felt like a Monday
after I left
the weekend was over, no more lazy
Sundays
Monday morning blues
that's what they call it
but when it lasts every day?
what do you call it?
love is too much work, I think I'll take a sick
day
and come back when your love doesn't feel
so...
Monday.

Spring 2010

I had a dream about you
nothing crazy this time
no missing fingers or teeth

we walked around the city
talking, laughing,
I don't remember what we were laughing
about but I remember it was hot

you always hated the heat
and still do
the curls tucked behind your ear were damp
with sweat

I twirled a lock of it around my finger just
because I liked touching you
and still do

then I wake up kinda sad because I had fun
then the memories come back and I get sad
again because
well, because we had some good times and
time moves too fast

so now all we have are photos and dreams of
way back when
when you hated the heat and I played in
your hair

but we also have each other
just different versions now
but I love you all the same
and the curly hair that grows in different
places now.

Sweet Oleander

Good girls bloom in the summer
plant my seeds in the winter
and I'll nourish you forever
honeysuckle sweet
sweet Oleander
a bouquet of love that lasts all year long
just add water

Jigsaw

I tried to think of a reason you'd ever be in a
jigsaw trap and nothing came to mind
I thought of reasons I'd be in jigsaw trap and
it would probably be because I call out of
work too much
or I was depressed that one day
Like that one guy in the first movie
and that other one
(Yes that actually happened)
The tape auto plays and the sounds of
muffled static talk to us in riddles
I can't follow because there are no subtitles
but all I can think about is how you got here
In this abandoned warehouse bathroom
where I can feel the mold multiplying on the
marble tile floors
I'm disgusted
That you're here in this place when there
must be a mistake
You never call out of work
Or forget to put the little twisty tie back on
bread bags
You even take the pack of ground beef back
to the meat department so it doesn't spoil
sitting in isle six.
You helped an old lady grocery shop
because she couldn't reach the top shelf
I can't think of any reason you'd be in a
jigsaw trap

So why are you here?
Maybe that's my punishment and this is my
game
not yours
Because even if we had to play a game for
survival you'd just let me win
You always do.

Amor de Colombia

The way the wind blows west
reminds me of you
a whisper brushes against my ear
humming the sweet serenade of music you
played for me
trumpets blaring loudly
as the sidewalks rumble under me
louder than the colors that cover the walls
of bold blues, lavenders, and greens
a morning glory that blooms in the summer
its heart shaped leaves and trumpet shaped
flowers
an honor it was to know you
a privilege to bask in your beauty
Cartagena
an ode to a beautiful, timeless city

Freedom Ring

It's tough
living in a country that bleeds red
when your blood bleeds blue
listening to the struggles of my ancestors
sung to me by a faceless man in a suit
he has no name
we just call him white supremacy
we were never really free
just given complimentary autonomy as a
treat
but ain't shit free
in this country of mine
we pay with our pride
our dignity
our honor
the blood of our sons, daughters, mothers
and fathers.

Homelander

Homelander desperately needs to be loved
by everyone around him or he'll spiral
it's either love him or fear him
the human race is in an abusive relationship
with Homelander
starlight is in an abusive relationship with
Homelander
he is a neglected child in a grown man's
body
homelander's relationship with Stormfront
was the only time he ever felt loved
anytime he loses a woman he feels entitled
to

He spirals

Madelyn
Stormfront
Becca
all dead

He spirals

Homelander isn't a person
he's a defective product
always mourning the mother he never had

A lot of men are Homelander

Desperately searching for their mothers in
evey woman they drain
desperately trying to overcomphensate while
being loathed by every woman they date

But they convince themselves they are
heroes in our story
saving us from the woes of the world
but the only woe is them
Victms of a system that they help to uphold

Love him for fear him

A defective product

A lot of men are Homelander.

My Little Shop of Horror

If you were a plant
you'd be a Venus fly trap
caring for you is too much work
your roots are too sensitive
too much dirt
too many rules
you've devoured so much
and I just don't have the time
to give you what you want.

Songbirds

Songbirds fly south for the winter
making homes in our hearts
setting nests in the windows
from treble strings in spinet pianos
I hear the music
the vibrato swims through my bloodstream
I can see myself in the water
my reflection, I think I knew her
I think about what life will be like once all
the birds are gone
their nests, empty
the music fading out
that nest in the window now holds empty
shells of me
who I used to be
I wonder when songbirds fly south for the
winter
can the ones they left behind, hear the music
still?
the melody
If I ask a songbird to stay behind when
winter's over,
Will she still sing for me?

LOVE

Long ago I thought
I didn't know what love was
a passing thought, I was
now I can feel it's joy
love.

Burning

Gatekeepers of love
the gods know I lust for you
my forbidden fruit
just one bite of you
now I'm in eternal pain
sent to hell for good.

Messages

Tucked beneath the jagged rocks
secrets lie in between
glass bottles with messages of lost lovers
too withered to read
I wonder what they say.

The Beach

Endless waters
mindless wonders
the tide is rolling in
love won't wait forever
don't think
just swim.

Tropical

Mango trees
leaves so green
so smooth
gliding across my fingers with ease
so rich & pure
like new love
fresh from the root.

Land Unsung

Humid Sun
a land unsung
let me sing it to you
a hymn for the arts
the culture
the sun
let me bring it to you
from my lips to your ears
we can indulge together, for years
forever.

Domme of my Subconscious

Restraints could never scare a girl like her
she eats leather & chains for breakfast
she is
an anomaly
a rebel with an appetite for chaos
she is
the one who keeps you up at night
she is
the master of your rapture
she knows what you like
she owns you
but you like it.

Their Eyes

At a distance they come in
others sail forever, never landing
that is the life
women don't want to remember
they don't want the truth
this woman eyes wide open
the sun was gone
but footprints on porches
tongueless, earless, eyeless
she ain't enough
she sits high, looks low
rocking forward, she spoke
we all know no woman past 40 and powerful
Sounds passed through
they set, seeing the woman
the envy chewed up
back parts and burning statements
killing laughs, mass cruelty
words without masters in a song
dat blue satin dress
all dat money
dat ole 40 year ole hair swingin'
betcha she don't stay.

Life Between the Pages

I self-isolate who I am
between pages and section breaks

colloquial and silver-tongues
maybe if I write enough
the tides will come

and wash away life as we know it
I'll be a new girl
then they'll be a new world

where the masks comes off
and I can breathe again
if I'm still here

and if not
I'll still be here
watermarked.

Black Culture

Ain't no culture like mine
black culture
we evolve with the times
but our essence never dies
different flavors of the same vibe
creating new and innovative ways to make
our souls thrive
everyone wants to be us
they want a taste of what we got
dipping their fingers in our sauce when they
can't even stir the pot
can't season meat
can't clean collards either
but expect cook out invites when they get a
little flavor
I think NOT
check your privilege at the gate
we'll bring you a plate outside.

Death Between the Pages

Sometimes I feel useless
and I don't know where these words come
from
but I know they come

when depression feels like dying under the
moonlight
when depression feels like taking your last
breath and tasting the stars

sometimes I feel like
these words are all I have
so I etch them onto my skin
so you can etch them onto my grave

and my last words can be some pseudo black
girl emo feminist shit
because that's who I am.

The Morning

I can't wait to wake up in the morning
and tell you about my crazy-ass dreams.

roll over and throw my arms on you
and spill all my anxieties into you
that come to me in the form of dreams.

but these aren't just any dreams
where Im back in DC but my mother is
Viola Davis
and my daddy is Chris Evans
and my sisters are still my sisters but not my
sisters?

if that makes sense, just hear me out while I
make sense of what I just saw while you
were sleeping
I was sleeping too, I think

I remember lying in bed and you called me
from the bathroom
and your hair was pink
I laughed, then I realized I was dreaming but
I couldn't wake up.

so I went back to sleep
and woke up to loud banging sounds then I
woke up again.

then I started shaking
then I woke up again
and this went on for what felt like an hour
then I felt you next to me

and I knew I was awake for real
because your touch lets me know I'm safe
and the nightmare is over
for now.

An Ode to Black Childhood

An ode to 99cent pickled eggs
smashed together in a sandwich bag of
ranch-flavored sunflower seeds

an ode to pickles
and penny candies
and pink starbursts whose wrappers littered
the ground

beneath us as we talked for hours
smacking our lips
and cracking our mouths as we smiled and
laughed at our own jokes

an ode to the old lady whose blind dog
freaked me out
every time I came through to buy my
pickled eggs
and pickles
and penny candies

sometimes I wonder if that house is still
there.
If the old lady's spirit still sits in front of that
tv
while the spirit of her blind dog waits for us
to come by one last time

an ode to my childhood

for I can't imagine a time
when things will ever be as simple as they
were back in the hood
when my only worries were which flavor of
sunflower seeds I wanted to suck the life out
of before spitting out what was left of the
good ol' days
on to the concrete

an ode to black childhoods
an ode to the streets.

Y'all Niggas

don't be caring about black women's plight
enough for me

y'all niggas don't be fighting the fight
enough for me.
screaming "Say her name!" Enough for me.
checking your rapist homeboys enough for
me.

loving dark-skinned black women enough
for me.
y'all niggas just don't work hard enough to
dismantle white supremacy enough for me.

because you don't want equality to want
privilege.
to sit on your high horse of patriarchy while
you look down on us and say "You bitches
ain't light enough for me."

"you don't mind your nigga enough for me."
"you ain't submissive enough for me."

that's why I really don't fuck with you
cishet niggas.
you don't be caring about nobody but
yourself and that shit just don't sit right with
me.

Love on a Dancefloor Memory

We moved together, him and I
as one under the dim lights on the dance
floor

I rested my cheek on his silk shirt
that smelled like sandcastles and ocean
water
the scent that reminded me of our nights at
the pier

my hands draped over his shoulders
my eyes gazed over at the exit door
the music became muddled like water in my
ears

I wish this night could last forever
I wish this soundtrack to our love would
never end.

My Love, My Morning Routine (Prose Poem)

In the morning, the sounds of the Keurig brewing wake me up from my sleep. He calls my name from the kitchen to ask if I want a cup. I say yes. I lay on my back because the bed leaves me sore. He walks in, I sit up, and he hands me my cup. "Day's like today, I wish I weren't a muggle." That's what my cups says. He knows me so well. He gives me this mug all the time because days like today are every day. I drink my coffee as he rubs my shoulder, asking if I slept good. I say yes. But yes is a lie. My right arm still hurts, and my chest is tight. My body is a mess, but this cup of hot coffee makes it all better. It's warm and inviting and gives me hope for the day. Those fifteen minutes before my coffee goes cold are honestly the best fifteen minutes of my day. After that, there is nothing to keep me warm on the inside. The rest of the day just drags. To be honest, I don't remember much about my day most days. Just when it's time to go to bed, and he rubs my shoulder again. And kisses me goodnight. And I drift off to sleep, looking forward to that morning cup of coffee again.

Black Lives STILL Matter

No justice, no peace
black trauma lives rent-free
in our heads

rent-free
no running water

rent-free
no healthcare
no money for bread

we'll starve
unless we lick the crumbs from the feet of
white supremacy.

Spring 2011

The floral print of my dressing gown
reminds me of a time
when the sun always shined

the warmth of love
covered my face

and nothing
but the smell of cherry blossoms
mattered to us.

My Stories Inside Me

I create people from liquid toners and
cellulose fibers
I give them afro-centric names and make
them dance for me
Perform their pain and joy for me. They tell
me all their secrets and I promise to keep
them between us
But I don't
While they sleep, I plot my next move
I take their pain and happiness and tell the
world their secrets
I profit from the pain of others. Putting our
pillow talk in between a 5x8 and stitched
binding
After a while, I get bored of them and need
new bodies to fill my void
 So I pull out my ingredients and get back to
work

Blackness Outta This World

Sometimes I sit and think what other planets
are like
If black people exist
If the teens have their own versions of the
hood where the girls eat hot chips and play
hand games
Mamas yell from blocks away to come
home before the street lights come on
A planet where water flows through every
neighborhood, produce grows in abundance
no matter the season and everybody gon'
eat
Everybody gon' succeed
Even this planet's version of Pookie got his
GED
If this planet exists, I hope they're doing
good
Sincerely, I hope they're happy.

Throughout the Years

The moments we share becomes an endless
loop
we communicate through Dixie cups with a
hole in the middle

no strings attached
but somehow we make it work
I make space, just a little

for you to hold my hand
while we figure out the world together.

Streams at Dawn

Rainfall in the morning
fill the streams at dawn
you fill me with so much joy
I can feel the water fill my heart
and nourish my soul

love slows down to where the river begins
a soft blue reflecting the sky
turns clear when it touches my toes
my skin shines

and I can't tell if my body is wet from the
rain
or from you

but I know that nothing compares to the
rain
and how it resembles our love
soothing, serene, and soft.

The World

I can't give you the world, but I can lasso
the moon
grab the stars on my way down
 so when you go to bed at night
your heart is full of milky ways and big
dippers
all the things that make your world shine.

A Pandemic Poem

If it weren't for miss Rona,
I'd be soaking up sun poolside
with a pina colada in one hand
and a mountain breeze gliding across the
other

instead, I'm soaking up sun under a palm
tree near the courtyard
of my apartment complex
with a phone in one hand and a pen in the
other

I can't go on vacation but I can write into the
void about it
that counts for something, right?

it means I can still feel
it means that I'm alive
and life's most precious moments never truly
die.

A Girl Without a Face

Even as I sit on my patio writing this poem,
there is a man staring at my breasts
even as I sit in the comfort of my own space
I'm still not safe from the world's misogyny
no woman is
no matter where we go there will always be
a man looking at our breasts while we talk
listening to us speak through our body parts
if he's even listening at all
I wonder if I wrote these lines with the tip of
his dick
would he stop staring then?

Ghosts in a Dream

Life is fleeting
death is promised

the invitation comes as a reminder in my
dreams
enough blood to wash over a city
and bring it to its knees

begging for mercy to live another day
spirits watching from windows
their faces, a ticking clock
their hands outstretched and cold
but I'm not ready to go

so back into the shadows they go
and I wake to another day
of life's open-invitation to the death
jamboree.

A Bountiful Feast of Flowers

Blueberry roses
melt like sugar beneath the concrete
 strawberry daffodils
lemon-flavored tulips
 grow like wild seed that couldn't wait to rise
up from nothing
just so they could see the beauty of life that
is you.

My Map of Inspiration

I wrote poems on the beaches of Colombia
with my toes in the sand
sonnets spilling from my pen.

it's a privilege to prose from across the
ocean
picking the fruits of my mind
an abundance of exaltation and tranquility

art that will never spoil
the memory of experience keeping it ripe
beauty and culture of new places serve as
inspiration
the mind must feel what it's like

to watch the natives dance in their
customary dress
the mind must feel how the savory spices
dance on the tongue
and unfamiliar music parades through our
ears

I wrote poems on the beaches of South
America
because I wanted the memory of how the
sand felt on my toes
to last forever.

You can't fight the beast
you can't control it's fury
but you can love him.

Your love feels foreign.
a language I don't speak
"oui." Speak it to me.

Days without sunlight
you left my soul wide open
then the rain came back.

So softly, touch me
just like you're not supposed to
screw the God's decree.

Skin flushed poppy red
the foliage underneath
sheds when you touch it.

Skin, soft like aster
tell me your favored flower
so I can have her.

Sand beneath my feet
the tide rolls in, the ships fleet
you sail away, free.

Honey

Your soul tastes like honey
not the pure, straight from the comb kind
but the altered, artificial, processed and
expired at the store kind
i never liked honey before you.
it was always too sweet for me
too thick
I'd dabble in a taste and my mouth would
recoil
but then you came along, and your honey
was different
so smooth and rich
a natural sugar rush that got my taste buds
tingling
so warm and inviting, the perfect remedy
but after a while, the taste got stale
what once glided across my tongue
now gets stuck on my gums
I can't put in my tea
on my toast
not even in my oatmeal
I've heard that if you keep it sealed
it can last a thousand years
maybe that's what I should've done
maybe I would still like you
maybe you would still be here

#GrowingUpBlack

Is season-all in your noodles for extra flavor
pretending to be a corner boy with your
bubble gum pager
weekends at granny's house with all 208 of
your cousins
hot combs on the stove
burning the backs of our necks for Easter
aunties home remedies
drinking ginger ale by the liter
double dutch
jump ropes smacking the pavement
Sunday dinner
soul food galore
staring at your mama's work in amazement
growing up black is...
the one thing that keeps us all connected
we are one.

WAP

Electric Slide across the Big Dipper
Harlem shake your way across Orion's Belt
Go On Girl!
 Twerk your way into another Universe
where black women's bodies aren't political
discourse
 Black and brown asses make the front
page news
like this planet ain't got enough problems
 babies starving in Beruit
but Bob and Bill from Fox News want to
know why Cardi B is twerking in a G-
string
 police terrorized impoverished
neighborhoods
but presidents want to know why Meghan
Thee has her fat ass on their son's TV
 for the life of me, I don't understand
why these folks so hot and bothered
 but I know another place exists,
somewhere
across the stars of Cassiopeia
Where we can be raunchy and
unconventional
with agency.

Tongue Tied

I wanna tell you my secrets
I want you to know what i hide
behind these brown eyes, lies
snippets from my past
lies that i tell
to keep up this false sense of happiness
like everything is okay between us
but there are cracks between us that can't be
fixed now
i wish we could be what we've always
wanted
but as long as my love for you is haunted by
whatever it is
then it is
what it is.

Love Language

My love language is art
derived from the Latin word *"ars"*
using your gifts to make this world ours
I get off on your skill, your craft
the things you can do with your hands
turning greys and greens into sage
telling stories through a glass lens
of night turning to day
giving life to blank pages
blank faces have a name, who didn't before
I get goosebumps in places I didn't before
I can lay up all day
and indulge in the art you create
it satisfies me in all the right ways.

She takes five steps back
Two steps forward to reach it
One step, and its gone.

An Ode to Moesha Mitchell, The Poet, and Angela Davis

I was watching an episode of Moesha and in
one scene she described herself as a poet, a
journalist, and Angela Davis. And in that
moment I realized WOW, I was a lot like
Moesha Mitchell.
My entire life I've been told that I'm a lot. A
lot like my mother, like most Black women
who demand to be heard and seen. I imagine
the universe was stirring a big ole' pot of
greens
and in that pot—a splash of determination
40 ounces of innovation
mixed together and tossed into a bowl of
collapsing stars.
And it created the black hole that is the
black woman.
We are far from a monolith, but the
similarities and connections we share are
unmistakable. Undeniable. Unattainable.
I guess anyone can do what we do, yet NO
ONE can do what we do.
So in a way, you could say, that being a
black, femme, feminine-presenting, always
venting about our traumas, black woman is
an Ode to Moesha. Because she was right.---
I too am a poet, a journalist and Angela
Davis.

White walls
eggshell while
cracks, like the delicate girl that I am.

Like Them

When I was little
I wanted hair like the white girls
skin like the white girls
eyes like the white girls
now I scroll these apps
just to see my features hijacked by the white
girls
who want to be black girls
but not the ones like me
the ones with the loose curls
who look like white girls
with a black daddy
and a white mama
I roll my eyes and swipe left
girl, ain't that some shit?
black is the new white girl

Violets

I am a flower
I know what I am
but what's the point in being one
if I'll never bloom?
never feel the sunlight of Sunna on my face
never feel the warmth of spring rain on my
skin
I am just a bud
stuck in a patch of heteronormative mud
the mud sticks to my legs and I try to crawl
out
but the rain that's meant to nourish me and
feed my roots just makes it worse
maybe I'm not a flower at all, but a weed
too aggressive and invasive wilting all the
authentic flowers around me
maybe my sole purpose is to produce little
seeds that become submerged and stuck in
the system maybe I don't deserve sunlight at
all
some flowers bloom just to get cut at the
stem
and placed in a vase
I used to think getting picked was the goal
but that's not the case
A flower is meant to stay, and live a full life
in her true form
attached to her roots
turns out I was a violet all along.

Symptoms of You

Feelings of euphoria
increased energy
lack of sleep
hunger
irritability
increase in sex drive
decrease in sex drive
swelling in the eyes, hands, or feet.

Cosmic Lust

In 1977 scientists received a WOW signal
near the constellation Sagittarius
The mouth of a woman outstretched,
sending waves of pleasure across the
universe
You know what they say about a Sagittarius
We're tough on the outside but soft like
silkworm underneath
The entire sequence lasted 72 seconds
And to this day, no amount of man's
research has been able to fully explain this
femme phenomenon
Many men have searched for this mystery
woman but the WOW signal was never
detected again
What an experience that must've been
Flirting with the unknown, an extraterrestrial
fling that was never going to pick you
but that didn't stop them from returning to
Big Ear hoping she would reach out again
Now 46 years later, astronomers believe that
the mysterious signal was from a distant,
sunlike star
And was never a woman at all
So they made her small
irrelevant
A footnote in the history books
Maybe one day she'll reach out again
But I don't blame her if she doesn't

Nobody likes a man that begs.

For Them (a tribute poem to my fictional FMC's)

This poem is for Darlene
who missed out on love in the form of a
Ford Anglia and sun-kissed red hair.

For Amanita who looked into the eyes of
death one too many times.

For River, who just wanted
a ruben sandwich on rye and got a taste of
blood instead.

For Amari, who knew what it felt like to be
submerged in the soil of pain until love
showed her the beauty of the flowers that
came after, and what they truly smelled
like.

This poem is for every daughter i gave birth
to in the form of a word doc.

This poem is for every girl who read a story
and saw herself like i see myself in
everything that i create.

This poem is for us.

11:11

A nightmare feels like a punishment for
longing
for those who dare to dream out loud and
without fear

a subconscious reaction to
gaslighting ones self into depression

you awake in an icy chill of panic, heart
pounding against your ribcage as your turn
and see the clock
it reads 11:11

eleven-eleven
a sign from the universe to keep
on dreamin'

Keep on hustlin' and let that paralyzing sleep
demon keep on sleeping on you.

F*cked

There is no consent under fascism.
no body autonomy in a place that owns you.
you lie back and take it,
while he strokes the freedom from your hair.
holds you down by the wrists
and whispers "How do you like this white
dick?"
when it's over, you clean yourself up
he counts his money
Self-righteous and placid
he gets what he wants
and you don't get shit
ain't got shit
won't ever have shit
not under this nation
ran by the good ol' boys and the capitalists
a revolution is coming, I feel it
won't be long now
your time will come
no more being fucked by fascism
we will rise, we will end it
together.

Coffee

Your love is patient
patience is key
your love is milk
i'm coffee
i like it hot
i like it sweet
fill me up
whip cream please
we're almost done
your cup is empty
i want a refill
extra sugar
a venti, hot drip
here's your tip
but before I take a sip
i wanna know
how you liked my coffee?

Hope Can Eat Later

In my dream she screamed
right in front of me
my anxiety, fear of the unknown stretched
across scrolling back
and wishing me a farewell
my nerves found humor in me
a gag gift
but she was wrong
I reached over equipped with myself and
was good enough
kicking off soft vibrations through my body
in my head
I walked outside I looked around
my dark skin, thick hair
awestruck coming among them
I heard a voice in my direction
my welcome
her grasp gently grabbed my worry
I was setting in
I was real
I peered at my surroundings
in an unfamiliar place
my native language holding my hand
hope can eat later.

The Color Purple

Move from the well
be ready
be cold
say nothing
hold her hand
don't leave, don't go
I don't know what else to say
I say kill this one too
never tell a good girl a sign is happening
spring come fussing too soon
he leave
can't you see that hurt?
git used to it.

Hello. If you're reading this, then that means you've gotten a copy of my, re-edited, refreshed and republished edition of my first poetry collection.

This book, is a combination of my first and second collection of poems. I started writing poetry in 2020, right before the covid pandemic hit and changed life as we know it. Both of my first collections, *'Sweet Oleander'* and *'I Had a Dream About You'* were written and released that same year. So many of my earlier poems were more of an experiment, than a representation of who I am—or was. Some of them were written as a personal challenge, while I figured out my voice as a poet. Even today, five years later, I'm still discovering my inner voice. A few of the poems featured in this updated collection, such as *'Passing' 'Their Eyes' 'Hope Can Eat Later' 'Anatomy of a Poem' 'Coldest Winter Ever'* and *'Cosmic Lust'* are new poems written within the last two years, that I included as a treat and to show my progression as a written and spoken word poet.

Thank you for buying or borrowing my book, and supporting my dreams.

-Love, Chanel Hardy

JOIN OUR
PODCAST!

You've done all this hard work! Now share with us! Email us at **cwwmagazinestaff@gmail.com** to share your poems! Still too shy? Share on our blog instead!

About the Author

Poet and painter born and raised in the Washington D.C. area. She is the owner of COFFEE WINE & WORDS Literary Press/magazine, and author of 'My Colorblind Rainbow' and other YA novels that have made the 'In The Margins Award Long List' for YA fiction in 2018 and 2020. Chanel has worked as a freelance writer, literary blogger and written for publications such as Women and Words, 25 Hottest Indie Authors Artists Advocates 2020, and CulEpi. She has had her artwork featured in galleries with the City of Las Vegas and World Gem Art Gallery.

Thank you for reading!

Follow me on social media!

@chanel.is.painting

@coffeewinewords